The Perfect Church

THE PERFECT CHURCH

by

Donald Llewellyn Roberts

∞

CHRISTIAN PUBLICATIONS, INC.

Harrisburg, PA

Christian Publications, Inc.
25 S. 10th Street, P. O. Box 3404
Harrisburg, PA 17105

The mark of CP *vibrant faith*

ISBN 0-87509-267-5
Library of Congress Catalog Card Number: 79-56331

CONTENTS

I. Appraisal

The Perfect Church

Behold, a pilgrim and his family went forth to worship.

"Wow, Dad, this church is something else!"

"Yes, son, I knew that they did things differently around here from back home, but a church shaped like a sycamore tree is something else. It really gets your attention."

Pilgrim and his family made their way to the entrance in the sycamore-shaped church. "You can understand why the building is so designed," observed Pilgrim. "It provides all this extra parking space underneath so some people don't have to go out in the rain."

Pilgrim and his family rode up the escalator toward the sanctuary. Busy ushers enfolded them with hospitality. As first-time visitors, the Pilgrims were duly marked with variegated stickers. By the time they were seated in cushioned style, they had almost as many seals as the Book of Revelation.

A brightly dressed "Wing Captain" sat down beside

them and quizzed them some more. You couldn't go unnoticed in this church. Pilgrim really did question having to give his blood type to the man, but the way it was explained, it was for emergency purposes. There had been cases when people had to be carried to the modern infirmary on the third floor for transfusions.

"Well," thought Pilgrim, "maybe I should get some information, too." "How long has this church been here?"

The Wing Captain was quick to answer. "Chapel of the Winns was founded about ten years ago on this former site of an orchard. The chapel has simply exploded since then."

"Chapel of the Winds. I like that. Do you have prevailing winds through this area?"

"Not winds, Winns! Dr. Wyatt W. Winn is the founder, and his seven sons assist in his ministry, especially since he's away at conferences about fifty weeks in the year. You've seen him on TV, haven't you? Winndows of Faith has become a popular program."

Why did you build a church shaped like a sycamore tree?" asked Pilgrim.

"First of all to relate to our humble origins in this orchard, then as a constant invitation to all sinners like Zacchaeus that they are welcome here, and also to provide handy parking for our numerous staff members. Did you meet our Parking Lot Pastor? He's a converted used car salesman. He groups people together by type of car, and creates a togetherness before they even enter the chapel."

"Is that Dr. Winn coming out on the platform?" questioned Pilgrim.

"No," responded the Captain. "Dr. Winn is in the Holy Land this week. That's the Minister of Preaching. You won't hear a finer message than he gives. He works very closely with the Minister of Sermon Research who spends all his time in the study preparing sermons; he's been here eight years now, but few people even know what he looks like. But this process frees up our preaching man for advanced studies and teaching in the local university."

"What do Dr. Winn's seven sons do?"

"The Doctor is grooming them for key posts here at the chapel, but right now they work behind the scenes with administration and finances. With the size staff we have and the amount of money involved, it takes a lot of managing. That's why we formed the Consortium of Church Management. Dr. Winn and his sons make up the Consortium. We call it 'The Board of Winners.'"

With that, the blast of twelve trumpets announced the opening of the service. Pilgrim and his family sat in hushed awe as the service began. The music was unreal as, in turn, the Ministers of Organ, Choir and Instrumentation took turns in pouring out a surge of anthems such as the Pilgrims had never heard before.

Even the twenty minutes taken by the Pastor of Public Relations to point out highlights of the week from the 16-page church bulletin could not detract from the flow of the service. They later learned that he was a converted disk jockey.

Everything built up to the sermon which issued forth from the Minister of Preaching as if it were his very own. Pilgrim and his family sat transfixed. Never had they seen things done in such a fashion. Their church back home seemed so crude and unpolished compared to all of this.

But the culmination of it all came as the invitation hymn was sung, accompanied by the massive chancel orchestra. The orchestra was located on a circular platform that rotated like a giant lazy susan, so that all the artists had equal front stage time.

As the invitation began, Pilgrim heard a strange whirring sound coming from the aisle, and was amazed to see the carpet moving. Beneath it a conveyor belt had been set in motion, and respondents rode down in a uniform and orderly pattern to be assigned by the Minister of Counselling to the right room. As the inquirers stepped off the conveyor belt, they were festooned with new sets of colored stickers. It seemed to Pilgrim as if a walking rainbow of humanity was flowing across the front of the auditorium. He genuinely wanted to be thrilled with all of this tangible response, yet deep inside he wondered if it wasn't too polished and mechanical and orderly. But then who was he to argue with success?

After the service, Pilgrim and his family were led by smiling hostesses into the Coffee Hour. Pilgrim struck up a conversation with a bright young man whose button indicated he was one of the welcomers.

"What happens to all of these people who come forward?"

"Well," came the answer, "they have to fill out cards which are then fed into the computer back at headquarters. From there, our professional Corps of Communicators process the cards and assign them to Vigilance Units for contact. Ultimately, all of these cards return to the Minister of Statistics who uses them to make projections on future growth trends for the chapel."

Pilgrim looked a bit wistful, then spoke: "It all sounds so efficient and organized. When something gets this big, don't you lose touch with the people?"

"Sir," said the welcomer, with an edge to his voice, "when your goal is outreach and a multi-thousand member church, you have to make certain sacrifices. Besides, our Corps of Communicators assign new people into groups we call 'A Winner's Circle,' and that seems to be doing the job. And look around. Ten years ago, this was just an orchard, now it's all of this. You just can't argue with success."

"But to get back to your question. All of these inquirers will have their cards screened by the Minister of Statistics who, in turn, will pass them on to the staff of the Minister of Seminars. That's when they begin their intensive training in every facet of life and churchmanship. The whole curriculum was prepared by Dr. Winn and is called 'Winn's Wisdom.' "

"Where do all of these thousands of people come from?" asked Pilgrim.

"Well, many are attracted by our wide use of the media, but we have also come upon an exciting new method to reach people. We have discarded our fleet of buses, and are now airborne. Did you see the big spread we received in *Tame* magazine last month on our 'Operation Cop-In'? We are the only church in the country using squadrons of helicopters to bring in people to church and Sunday school from as far away as 70 miles. Our Minister of Aerial Education has installed overhead projectors in the copters for teachers while flying back and forth to the chapel. The logistical problems our Minister of Transportation faces are immense. We have called this effort 'Winn's Whirly-birds.' This will help us fulfill Dr. Winn's dream of a larger building he wants to leave behind him as a memorial. It will seat 144,000."

"Wow," said Pilgrim. "This is simply mind-boggling. No wonder our church back home never exploded. We must not have had any vision. Oh, it's getting late, and we need to be heading for home."

Clutching her $6.95 copy of Dr. Winn's autobiography, *Winning Is the Name of the Game*, Mrs. Pilgrim seemed utterly subdued.

What was there left to say after such an experience of worship? And how could anyone argue with success?

The Current Issues

HAVING JUST ALLOWED ourselves the luxury of an imaginary encounter with a "perfect" church, we must now return to reality. The serious-minded recognize that there is no such thing as a perfect church, be it in or out of the Scriptures. The epistles were written to a great degree to redress problems in local churches. There is no room for dreamy-eyed idealism in the New Testament. But if one uses the word perfect in terms of mature or fruitful, one could allow for a moving toward that kind of perfection. Even so the human dimension always brakes any arrival at literal perfection.

Although Christians in America would hesitate to pin the label of perfect on a group or an individual congregation, they are oriented toward the success syndrome. Thus, a going operation with escalating size reflected in staff, statistics, and shekels ranks high in modern day thought as to what constitutes perfection.

The mythical, though recognizable, church of the preceding chapter poses in satirical form some serious questions about the Church. How efficient should a church be? Granted, there is no merit in pious chaos, but where is that fine line which distinguishes serving the Lord "decently and with order" and the drift into a mechanical reliance on mere methodology? Somewhere between lethargy and lunacy lies that balance of spiritual life with the precious touch of the human.

Is size the measure of real growth? Some, stratified in a dying fellowship of the same old faces, will take delight in lampooning numerical growth. Still the Book of Acts indicates a legitimate place for numerical increase. Yet, increased statistics bring increased problems, and may well divert a church from a meaningful ministry. Snyder's *The Problem of Wineskins* and Worley's *A Gathering of Strangers* point up some current problems in the attempt to correlate numerical and spiritual growth in the Church.

A highly crucial issue centers in the matter of professionalism. Certain segments of the Church today are trying to go in two directions at once, i.e. large staffs of professionals and increased emphasis on the utilization of spiritually gifted laymen. Parking Lot Pastors and Ministers of Public Relations are not all that far-fetched in the current quest for well-oiled ecclesiastical machinery. One might almost cry out for an occasional mispronounced word in a sermon or a missed choral note to ensure one's being in the presence of real people, and not robots.

Thus, the chapters which follow serve as an effort first to analyze some areas of need and then offer already known counsel. Since "repetition is the mother of learning," we must continue to rehearse these time-honored concepts from the Scriptures. Our churches often fall prey to modeling themselves after fads and falsely understood ideas of "success." Such need to be examined in terms of the Scriptures.

There is also an underlying concern throughout this book. It lies in the growing preoccupation in the Church with subjectivity, the yearning for experiences. Is this an unconscious fall-out from a world seeking highs from moral lows? The writer desires a return to the Pauline format, sound doctrine out of which wells practical experience. Today many seem to desire to hurdle over sound doctrine and plunge into religious experience alone. The history of the Church is replete with illustrations of what spiritual shipwreck such an approach has proven to be.

Lest some think at the outset that this volume is a call to mere stereotyped orthodoxy, it must be stated that in essence this is an effort to recall many to a healthy, biblical mysticism. That word need not frighten us, for it lights the way to wholesome biblically-rooted experience, that insatiable drive to know the Living God, as revealed through His Son Jesus Christ.

Under the heading of "Anomaly" emphasis is placed on: repentance; exposition of the totality of Scripture; a renewed emphasis on the presence of God; a concern for spiritual effectiveness; and the necessity for vital spiritual life. These concepts are contrasted with incipient trends in the Church today.

The section headed, "Antidote" offers more concrete

material on the importance of a sheep and Spirit-centered ministry in the local church, followed by means to achieve that end. "The Ears Movement" seeks a salutary answer to certain emphases by calling the Church to a listening stance in order that it might better know the will of God in service; and then a call to implement the drive to know God in a deeper and more personal way.

The epilogue is an exposition of the Book of Acts in terms of the repeated word "great," which word delineates for us, in biblical terms, the measure of true spiritual success and greatness in the Church.

II. Anomaly

Repentant or Recycled

THE RELIGIOUS SCENE today abounds with novelty.

The accent is on involvement, personal and group confrontation, dialogue, communal life, and sharing. Some Christians seem much taken with the street talk of love and peace and have emphasized this in ministering to others.

No doubt there is always danger in clinging to stereotyped methods from the past, but there is also danger in simply adopting modern patterns which have had a veneer of biblical truth applied.

Out of the present-day welter of novelty, certain observable results appear. One of them is subjectivity. The feelings of an individual toward God become significant. God's love alone is the preeminent biblical teaching of the new approach. People are pronounced Christians when they grant God a hearing and then respond to His love and beneficence to them.

Certainly all would agree with Paul that ". . .notwithstanding, every way, whether in pretense, or in truth, Christ is preached; and I therein do rejoice, yea, and will rejoice" (Phil. 1:18). Thus, we do well to flee the pharisaical narrowness which proscribes any person or thing which does not fit into our own little groove of reasoning.

But in the present theological climate, there is another Pauline pole of thought to remember: ". . .though we, or an angel from heaven, preach any other gospel unto you than that which we have preached unto you, let him be accursed" (Gal. 1:8).

Therein lies the key to the gospel. The key is objectivity. No matter what our emotional highs and lows, no matter what our feelings toward God may be in any set of circumstances, the gospel remains the same, a mirrored reflection of the eternal God "with whom is no variableness, neither shadow of turning."

This leads us to a very serious question relative to the new approach.

Though granting the sincerity of one who might offer the gospel in this context, still is there not a note missing? The objective teachings of Scripture, not sincerity, must always be the Christian's criterion for truth.

What is the missing note in the new approach to the gospel? It is the playing down, perhaps unwittingly, of the place of repentance in the declaration of the gospel to modern man.

How this has happened is very understandable. The generation which skips blithely past the geometric spiral of increasing crime and pronounces it a "sickness," the by-product of social environment, will hardly be the generation receptive to so biblical a concept as repentance.

Christians feel they must present the gospel in positive terms lest they create a negative image for Jesus Christ. Conversion thus becomes an acceptance of Jesus Christ, with hardly a ruffle to that inner Adamic nature the Scripture calls the flesh. Is modern man so fragile a creature that his conversion must be abetted with such conveyor-belt ease?

What does Scripture say? Our Lord spoke of the Holy Spirit's ministry as including reproving or convicting the world of sin (John 16:8), the sin of failing to believe on Him. Paul told the Thessalonians that salvation came "through sanctification of the Spirit and belief of the truth." This sanctification is twofold in nature: being rent away from what we were and being set apart to become a child of God through the new birth, receiving His nature in order to accomplish His will.

Conviction and rending are terms of action. Fallen men see, through the Word of God and the work of the Spirit, what they really are and how desperately they need Jesus Christ. The Scriptures describe such a holy violence as repentance.

What underlies the present-day shifting away from the preaching of repentance is a failure to declare a balanced view of God. God *is* love. He *is* merciful, gracious, and good. But He is also "a consuming fire," and the One who cannot look upon evil. Incarnate, the Lord Jesus Christ, so-called revolutionary to some and the epitome of peaceful meekness to others today, had twice as much to say about hell as heaven in His recorded words. Therefore, it is not how I feel about

God but how God feels about me that really counts.

God's feelings are objectively recorded in the Scriptures. It is not for man to enter into a dialogue with deity but rather to enter into discipleship, a relationship which must be preceded by repentance and faith.

There is a distinct sense in which the Scriptures are God's continued call to man to repent. It begins with His loving though firm question to Adam, "Where art thou?" It continues through His dealings with His people in the Old Testament and culminates in His closing interrogation in Malachi of the question-laden returnees from captivity.

If Moses, Isaiah, Daniel, Paul, and John and countless others in Scripture fell in weakness and awe in the presence of the eternal and holy God, where does arrogant, sophisticated modern man stand? He cannot have a genuine faith in Jesus Christ until he is told what God is like, and what he, man, is like. Only then, under the convicting work of the Holy Spirit, will he sense his need, recognize his sinfulness, be smitten with godly sorrow and grief over his sin and, with true repentance, turn to Calvary and the Lamb of God.

Modern man can scarcely afford any shortcuts to the cross. He must walk up the same narrow path all the saints have trod through the ages. We do him serious soul damage to offer anything less than what the Scriptures outline.

How significant is repentance in the New Testament? Repentance commands a very prominent place, especially in the emphasis upon it at several key junctures in the New Testament.

As John the Baptist, the forerunner and preparer for Christ, came preaching, what was the basic thrust of his message? Luke 3:3 records it as follows: ". . .he came into all the country about Jordan, preaching the baptism of repentance for the remission of sins." The context reveals that John singled out the chronic sins of the masses of people, as well as publicans and soldiers. The Preparer preached repentance.

Then when the Lord Jesus stepped from the shadows of obscurity into the full blaze of public notice, having been baptized and tempted, He came into Galilee preaching. What does the writer of Scripture record as His initial emphasis? "The time is fulfilled, and the kingdom of God is at hand: repent ye, and believe the gospel" (Mark 1:15).

Another significant New Testament signpost was established on that epochal occasion, Pentecost. In the midst of the supernatural manifestations and glorious events of Pentecost one tends to lose sight of this. The record is that when the guilt-stricken listeners cried out, "What shall we do?" at the close of Peter's Spirit-empowered message, the first word which fell from the lips of the apostle was "Repent" (Acts 2:37-38).

There is one final passage to consider. John recorded the messages of our Lord to the seven churches of Asia Minor. To the local church at Laodicea Christ gave a final specific word: "Repent" (Rev. 3:19).

There is no intent here to minimize the importance of faith as the positive reception of Jesus Christ as Savior and Sovereign. However, the language of Scripture is unmistakable concerning the high priority given to repentance in conversion. The illustrations above, coming as they do at such very crucial points in the New Testament, reinforce the thesis as to the importance of repentance.

No question about it, the Christian of the twentieth century is being pressed to re-examine his methods for communicating the gospel. He better appreciates today Paul's heart-cry, ". . .I am made all things to all men, that I might by all means save some" (I Cor. 9:22). But we need to be careful lest we be hypnotized with all this talk about how different and unique modern man is supposed to be.

What is needed today is a dogmatic flexibility. Flexible in the sense of Paul, as cited above, yet utterly dogmatic concerning the gospel message, and especially the absolute necessity for the continued and clear declaration of repentance, yes even to modern man.

It is not by chance that the Third Person of the Godhead is called the *Holy* Spirit. He cannot indwell any human being apart from a radical dealing with sin. If to some this sounds archaic, then we gladly run the risk of being out of step with current thought, so long as we are in step with the truth of the eternal God.

Let us be sure that in our desire to reach the Now Generation, we do not eviscerate the gospel by leaving out one of its integral parts—repentance.

Feast or Famine

"Behold, the days come, saith the Lord God, that I will send a famine in the land, not a famine of bread, nor a thirst for water, but of hearing the words of the Lord." These words were spoken toward the close of the ringing indictment of Israel by the prophet Amos, a fiery preacher someone has called "God's little lightning bolt."

That is, indeed, a strange and awesome thought—the possibility of a famine of the Word of God—and stranger still that it should occur among the very people to whom had been committed the oracles of God. Yet, for all of the modern translations of Scripture, printed Bible study helps, and tidal wave of literature on biblical themes, our own generation may also be suffering from a famine of the Word.

The editor of a Christian periodical recently suggested to his constituency that their churches might be producing biblical illiterates. He referred to youth and adults, exposed to years of church life in a distinctly Bible-oriented setting, who still remain tragically inept in their handling of the Word of God. A layman recently admitted that he felt utterly at sea with the Old Testament and then added significantly, "Somewhere along the line we should be made to learn about it."

Yes, somewhere along the line every Christian should serve an apprenticeship in the Word of God, and receive that basic grasp of its truths he needs for all the days of his life.

But the very churches which would shrink in horror at any questioning of II Timothy 3:16, "All Scripture is God-breathed," are the ones most in peril of substituting stones for the living bread of the Word. John Wycliffe, who gave the world its first complete translation of the Scriptures into the vernacular English, once alluded to a comment of William of St. Armour.

Observing the zeal of the medieval friars in extracting money in order to build monasteries, William had said, "The friars are worse than the devil; the devil proposed to turn stones into bread; the friars turn the bread of the poor into stones."

There is a real danger today that stones instead of bread are being offered to God's hungry sheep. An obvious situation appears in the growing orientation toward subjectivity in our churches. We have narrowed down our searching of the Scriptures to a minimal number of passages in a quest for experiences, to the exclusion of understanding the total sweep of Scripture. A broad understanding alone can give the perspective and balance needed to beget the kind of Spirit-directed experience God purposes for us.

Indeed, there is a frightening drift into subjectivity, and a whole new religious jargon has appeared to foster it. Dr. Addison H. Leitch, in his last published article in *Christianity Today*, wrote:

"The Spirit-filled Christian uncontrolled by the words of Scripture becomes wild—what Calvin called a 'frantic.' This is a danger in many charismatic movements today. It is also a danger in many enthusiastic youth movements where singing and 'sharing' crowd out the Scriptures."

Sharing has become a big word in the religious vocabulary today. But what is being shared? In many instances, ignorance. Bible classes and study groups have been turned into Christian sensitivity sessions where people simply talk about themselves and learn very little about the Word. Now, there is a place for personal exchange, but only as long as it relates to clear biblical instruction. People should go out with scriptural truth and principles to redirect their lives, not a mental maze of "what's happening?"

We preachers have not been faultless either, for far too much of current preaching is story time, and strings of illustrations, rather than sound exposition of the Word of God. Vance Havner wryly observed that "the saints now want to be amused, not amazed."

There is no excuse for catering to this modern craving for religious entertainment. Our orders are clear. We are to preach and teach the whole counsel of God, and not be swayed either by current fads or personal tangents.

The Church has also allowed the world to dictate its priorities, apparently fearful lest it be considered out of step with "relevant" issues. Why should we want to be in step with a system which Paul called "this present pornographic age" (Gal. 1:4)?

Dr. A. W. Tozer, indeed a prophet in the twentieth century, well observed, "Much that the Church—even the evangelical Church—is doing these days she is doing because she is afraid not to. The pressure of public opinion calls us, not the voice of God." But Dr. Tozer went on to offer a solution in his book *Of God and Men*:

"The Church at this moment needs men, the right kind of men, bold men. The talk is that we need revival, that we need a new baptism of the Spirit, but we languish for men of God, for prophets again in our pulpits instead of mascots. The glowworm has taken the place of the bush that burned and scintillating personalities now answer to the fire that fell at Pentecost."[1]

There is a famine of the Word today, a famine of solid biblical exposition and exhortation, with application built on sound doctrine. A new Galatianism stalks the land while the sheep are caused to graze in the pews on stories, sensationalism and strivings after instant spiritual maturity.

The prophet Amos took the Word of God back to the house of God. That's the need today. With King Josiah of old, Amos could well have used the sermon title, "Lost in Church: One Bible." The seventh chapter of

Amos suggests a man somewhat quizzical as he passed Jerusalem on the way to Bethel in Israel: Why would God use a rural fruit picker to straighten out the sophisticated set at the king's chapel?

But still he went, and in going, he brought the Word of God back to Bethel, the house of God. By modern standards, Amos was no great human success story, but he was successful in terms of obedience to the Lord.

Centuries later, the Apostle Paul made a similar appeal to the churches in the pastoral letters. He urged on Timothy and Titus the priority of preaching and teaching the full orb of biblical truths which alone could arrest error and invest believers with Spirit-born vitality and growth.

We desperately need men of the convictions of Amos and Paul, men weary of this preoccupation with experience-seeking, Satan-discussing, ignorance-sharing, and church-efficiency-making. We need an entire corps of such prophets to cause our churches again "to rejoice and blossom as the rose," as hungry hearts are filled with the content and conviction which only a total teaching of the Scriptures can give. For "The entrance of thy words giveth light; it giveth understanding unto the simple" (Ps. 119:130).

Our churches would do well to declare a moratorium on much of their feverish programming, and substitute a pattern such as Wycliffe's for his Lollards, that the Word of God might be mastered, and also be the master: "Obtain a reliable text, understand the logic of Scripture, compare the parts of Scripture with one another, maintain an attitude of humble seeking, and receive the instruction of the Spirit."

In this era of theological oversimplification, when far too many want experiential cream puffs, let spiritual meat again be offered from the pulpits and classes that a growing famine of the Word be arrested.

Let us be reminded of Dr. Tozer's spiritual rule of thumb, lost in these hectic days:

"No short cut exists. God has not bowed to our nervous haste nor embraced the methods of our machine age. It is well that we accept the hard truth now: the man who would know God must give time to Him. He must count no time wasted which is spent in the cultivation of His acquaintance."[2]

The Word of God cannot be absorbed by osmosis, neither can it be condensed into some pat formula. There is needed today a painful discipline, foreign to a permissive age, which alone can produce the delights of knowing and obeying God's Word. Solomon wrote of the man "who lacked nothing for his soul of all that he desireth. . .yet had not the power to enjoy it."

Let the famine of the Word be halted. Let the chaff be scattered by the wind of God, and let that holy breath of God once more be allowed to give us that balanced life-producing diet from the storehouse of truth, even the *entire* Word of God.

---

1. A. W. Tozer, *Of God and Men* (Harrisburg: Christian Publications, Inc., 1960), pp. 14, 15.

2. A. W. Tozer, *The Divine Conquest* (Old Tappan: Fleming H. Revell, 1950), p. 22.

Presence or Presents

SOME SIXTEEN AND A HALF centuries ago, the early Church waged a great theological controversy over the nature of Christ. The final decision of the Council of Nicaea actually hung upon one Greek letter. The Church today faces another crucial issue, an issue which hangs upon two English letters. Shall we be taken up with the *Presents* of God, what God gives, or shall we be primarily concerned about the *Presence* of God, who God is? The distinction is of great moment, for someone has well observed that the quality of the Church's life will very much reflect her understanding of the person of God.

The concern springs from a modern-day preoccupation with what God does for us. We do well to trace the background of this interest as Paul faced it in the Corinthian situation.

As Paul wrote the crucial Roman epistle from the city of Corinth, he first declared the basic indictment of the pagan world. Men outside the grace of God had changed both the glory of God and the truth of God

(Rom. 1:23, 25). No doubt, his day-by-day experiences in metropolitan Corinth confirmed the tragic evidences of this exchange.

Immediate consequences arose from this perverse transaction. Paul thrice writes that God "gave them up" (Rom. 1:24, 26, 28). The shade of meaning is fine. God did not give up on man, for the Cross was the constant reminder of His love, but He did give man up to what he desired. C. S. Lewis in *The Problem of Pain* comments on this: "The lost enjoy forever the horrible freedom they have demanded, and are therefore self-enslaved."[1]

But the underlying error crystalizes what Paul says of fallen men, that he ". . .worshipped. . .the creature more than the Creator, who is blessed forever. Amen" (Rom. 1:25). Things replaced Him! The creature was now to be taken up with the creation, rather than with the Creator. That is the glaring error of idolatry, no matter what the century may be!

This concern for the condition of fallen man may also have alerted the apostle to a similar situation in the Christian fellowship at Corinth. Serious enough that fallen man was preoccupied with the creation rather than the Creator, but was it not a sin of equal magnitude developing among the Corinthian believers?

Were they not becoming more concerned about the gifts than the Giver? First Corinthians 1:29 could well be a theme verse in this matter as Paul drew the contrast between the presents and the presence of God. Thus he wrote: "That no flesh should glory in his

presence," or "That all flesh might not boast before
him (God)." That the Corinthians were boasting in the
flesh is abundantly clear from the outset of the first
Corinthian epistle. The interest and the energy of the
fellowship was being misdirected away from the
source of "every good and perfect gift."

God had given to the church at Corinth *people*.
Called out ones, they were to be separated from the
gross brutality of a corrupted society unto the glorious
purposes of the Triune God. Collectively and person-
ally they constituted the Temple of God, fleshed out
habitations for the God who had called them to holiness, not uncleanness. Together they stood as a
tremendous potential when gifted and empowered by
the Holy Spirit. Sadly, they far too often reflected their
former clime of life and became man-centered.

The brethren began to choose up sides and faction-
alize the Body. First Corinthians 1 and 3 especially
reveal this. Whatever went into the particular
position, at least four groups emerged, three of them
oriented toward men, Paul, Apollos, and Cephas. The
fourth group might well have been the most dangerous
in piously claiming to be "of Christ."

Instead of being recognized as valuable additions to
the fellowship, individuals became points of controversy and division. The Corinthians were very subtly
changing the glory and truth of God into an idol called
man. The Church today is not guiltless at this point.
Far too much of the work of God is attributed to mere
men "who strut and fret upon the religious stage." Dr.
A. W. Tozer well capsulated this sad truth: "The

grosser manifestations of these sins, egotism, exhibitionism, self-promotion are strangely tolerated in Christian leaders even in circles of impeccable orthodoxy. Promoting self under the guise of promoting Christ is currently so common as to excite little notice."[2]

How frightening this preoccupation with men could become reveals itself in Paul's rebuke of the Corinthians for allowing their schisms to be injected into the precious fellowship about the Lord's Table. So serious was this viewed that God moved in anger, and caused physical judgment to fall upon some in the church. No man must glory in the presence of God!

Not only had the Lord blessed the Corinthians with the gift of people, but He also had given to them *power*. This power, expressed in authority and spiritual dynamic, was for the purpose of edification and evangelism to the glory of God. But again, a carnal and cultural flaw betrayed itself in the believers' approach to the *charismata/pneumatikoi*. They forgot, in their zest to find a place of prominence, that God had sovereignly dispensed these gifts. In His sight the gifts were essentially equal even as each member of the physical body had its place and function. The Corinthians, obviously conditioned by their past, began to single out certain gifts as being, they thought, the more significant ones. How little we learn from the past. The Corinthian error has exploded again in our times!

Paul spent three chapters of this epistle dealing with the problem. Apparently, the misunderstanding and abuse of the *charismata* had reached epidemic proportions. In fact, the entire Corinthian literature could well constitute a manual on "How Not to Conduct a Local Church Ministry."

There is a great resurgence of interest in the Church today in the subject of the gifts of the Spirit, and rightly so. Too long the Church languished with a mind-set that saw only professionals as competent to do the work of the ministry. Each member of the Body must function as directed of the Spirit. Yet again, the error of changing the glory and truth of God threatens, as now regenerate men become more preoccupied with the presents from God, rather than with the presence of God.

It should not be surprising to us that, in a culture so geared to appearances and instants, many in the Church in America are taken with the visible, the showy, the different. That Paul injected I Corinthians 13 into this controversy may well be to remind us all of a pivotal relationship between the fruit of the Spirit and the gifts of the Spirit. Spiritual power and giftedness are in ratio to control by the Spirit and the manifestation of His life, much in keeping with the teaching of John 15 and Galatians 5. So this instructive section in I Corinthians is in fact a rebuke since no man should glory save in the presence of God!

Mindful of this very subtle drift from center, the apostle sought to reorient these believers to the priority importance of the presence of God in their midst. Thus, Paul swept the spectrum of time to re-emphasize the meaning of the presence of God!

There was a *past presence*. God the Son, at precisely the right moment in history, had come forth. Clothed in flesh, yet apart from sin, He took up residence among His creatures, and finally tasted death for them—at their hands. He lived and ministered upon this planet revealing God in the flesh. But He came with the supreme purpose of offering Himself on the cross for the sins of the world. And, because He was God, that sacrifice needed to be made just once. Thus, Paul urged at the outset of the letter a great concern lest anything nullify or blunt the impact of the preaching of the cross (I Cor. 1:17).

There is also a *present presence*. God the Spirit had taken up residence in the lives of the redeemed. The temple of stone has now been replaced by living temples who can walk around, and take the personal presence of God everywhere. Mindful of that presence, Paul rebuked the fellowship at Corinth for sin, and reminded them that individually and collectively, they were the temple of God (I Cor. 3:16; 6:19-20). God was now in the midst of His people again, not in a tent of fabric, but in tents of flesh. Paul also reminded them of the importance of recognizing God's presence as they gathered about His Table. That warning needs to be sounded afresh in a time when the Lord's Supper has become an appendage to worship in far too many churches.

There will be a *future presence*. Scripture abundantly teaches a personal presence of Christ in returning and reigning upon this earth. Where He was rejected, there also He shall be recognized and honored

as King of Kings, and Lord of Lords. As Paul answered
the questions of the Corinthians about the nature of
the resurrection, he also conveyed forcefully the fact of
Christ's return (I Cor. 15:51-52). Having begun this
epistle with the thought of His return (I Cor. 1:7-8), so
the apostle closed with the words of I Corinthians
16:22, "Maranatha," "Our Lord, come."

We are too much taken with the presence of man
these days. Well has someone observed, "Nothing of
God dies when a man of God dies." He who moves in
the realms of eternity alone is indispensable. Men can
be replaced, and will be replaced, when they take to
themselves that glory which only God deserves.

The Church today needs the presents which God has
purposed for her blessing and ministry. But far more
keenly does she need a new sensitivity to the presence
of God. Only then can self-confident, eager Adams of
this century be cut down to workable size. We are too
much taken with the creature and not enough with the
Creator. We are slipping off onto tangents of preoccupation with our own plans and empires. The Church
needs to be touched afresh with the presence of the
holy Discomforter.

Instead of showing one another the glories of our
accomplishments for God, our generation needs the
heart-cry of Moses of old on that awesome mount.
There God answered his request and showed to Moses
as much of His glory as mere man could see and
survive. We should long for such a spirit again! Only
that constant touch with the presence of God can keep
in true perspective the presents from God!

1. C. S. Lewis, *The Problem of Pain*, (Scarborough: MacMillan Pub. Ltd., 1953), pp. 115, 116.
2. A. W. Tozer, *The Pursuit of God*, (Harrisburg: Christian Publications, Inc., 1948), p. 45.

Effective or Efficient

PEOPLE TODAY SEEM PREOCCUPIED with church efficiency. They want to know how to improve this or how to polish that or how to make the Church run so smoothly that it will purr like a well-tuned engine.

Often caught in the middle of this drive for efficiency, pastors are suddenly overwhelmed by the revelation that they and their congregations are inefficient.

But is efficiency the same as effectiveness? Elijah was extremely efficient on the mount in preparing the sacrifice, but the fire had to come down from God. Elijah's modern counterparts seem more concerned with having the neatest and the best sacrifices; but, unlike Elijah's case, nothing happens because there is no holy fire from above.

Efficiency is doing something in the right way. Effectiveness is doing something in the right way, with power—the power of God.

E. M. Bounds in *Power Through Prayer* writes: "The Church is looking for better methods; God is looking for better men. What the Church needs today is not more machinery or better, not new organizations or more and novel methods, but men whom the Holy Spirit can use. He does not flow through methods, but through men."[1]

We try to institutionalize what God does through a given life or church by packaging and wholesaling the same through seminars and workshops. But it's ludicrous, for example, for a church in northern Vermont to pattern itself after a work in southern California.

On at least three occasions the Old Testament records instances of disastrous dependency on something external, with a disregard for the fact that God blesses yielded lives, not instruments or procedures.

The Ark of the Covenant was a constant reminder to the Israelites of the promises of God, and of the very Shekinah Glory of God. But, in I Samuel 4, we find a people who had tolerated sin in the nation and the priesthood facing crisis times with the Philistines. Their reaction was ". . .Let us fetch the ark of the covenant of the Lord out of Shiloh unto us, that when it cometh among us, *it* may save us out of the hand of our enemies" (I Sam. 4:3).

The Ark of the Covenant had become a good luck charm. The result? "And the Philistines fought and Israel was smitten, and they fled every man into his tent: and there was a very great slaughter; for there fell of Israel thirty thousand footmen. And the ark of God was taken; and the two sons of Eli, Hophni and Phinehas, were slain" (I Sam. 4:10-11).

After many years God made Hezekiah king of Judah. The Assyrians, fresh from victory over the northern kingdom, threatened the very existence of the southern kingdom; but God gave Judah a temporary stay of execution for He used Isaiah and Hezekiah to move the nation back toward Himself. Thus, we read in II Kings 18:4, "He (Hezekiah) removed the high places and brake the images, and cut down the groves, and brake in pieces the brazen serpent that Moses had made: for unto those days the children of Israel did burn incense to it: and he called it Nehushtan."

One generation's blessing had become another generation's bane, when dependency on God was diverted to an object (the bronze serpent) related to God. The third illustration is the most awesome. The prophet Jeremiah (in the waning days of the southern kingdom) warned the nation that it was ripe for judgment. Many thought that God would never allow the Babylonians to defeat them. But Jeremiah said: "Trust ye not in lying words, saying, The temple of the Lord, The temple of the Lord, The temple of the Lord, are these" (Jer. 7:4). What he was saying was that not even the sacredness of the temple could save them if they failed "to amend" their ways. The prophet Ezekiel, in exile, had the sad task of explaining to fellow captives the step-by-step departure of the presence of God from the temple. There would be no premature return to the land. The seventy years would have to be fulfilled, and even the temple in Jerusalem would not be spared.

These three illustrations emphasize the fact that we must not depend on the externals. Not even the ark, the bronze serpent, nor the temple could insure automatic blessing. Nor can we program God. We can't squeeze Him into our mold, however sincere our motives.

God is not adverse to order and organization. The sacrificial system and the arrangement of the tribes about the tabernacle illustrate this in the Old Testament; directions concerning the Lord's Supper and order in the local church reveal organization in the New Testament. But the present generation of believers is so deluged with seminars and training sessions and preparations that they never get to practice what they learn.

When Paul admonished the Ephesian church to "Put on the whole armour of God, that ye may be able to stand against the wiles of the devil," the word he used for "wiles" could be transliterated into English as "the methods" of the devil. One of Satan's methods is to get us leaning on methods instead of on the Spirit of God.

Vance Havner has observed, "Never before has the Church had so many degrees yet so little temperature." Rather, we need the positive affirmation of the Apostle Paul, "For this cause also thank we God without ceasing, because, when ye received the word of God which ye heard of us, ye received it not as the word of men, but as it is in truth, the word of God, which effectually (with energy) worketh also in you that believe" (I Thess. 2:13).

Today's emphasis seems to be drifting from the

Word of God to the worker for God; from the breath of God to the brains of humanity; from the Mighty Servant, our Lord, to the micro means of men. But if we are to reach men and women for Jesus Christ, we must depend on the Spirit alone.

The story of David underlines this need. As David took a stand for God against Goliath, he received all sorts of advice relative to weaponry and strategy. Had he lived in our era, he might have been sent to a cram session on "Basic Giant Conflicts" or a seminar on "The Cultural Disadvantages of Encountering Philistines." But David, in his simple faith, refused the armor and the sword of Saul saying, "I cannot go with these; for I have not proved them." What a commentary on today's scene.

Instead David took his sling and the five smooth stones, and to the dismay of all the experts, slew Goliath. David was simply himself—in the hand of God.

We must not be content with mediocrity, but we also must avoid becoming the mass-produced products of the experts. If we pursue any expert, let that expert be God.

Let's use efficiency only as a supplement to God's effectiveness as given by His Spirit for His work.

As we reject the shoddy in our service for God, so we must also reject slavish adherence to simplistic formulae espoused by experts. Expertise in the quest for the Lord should be our goal.

---

1. E. M. Bounds, *Power Through Prayer*, (Grand Rapids: Zondervan Publishing House, 1974), pp. 11, 12.

Living or Large

THE SELDOM CONSIDERED EVENT of the ascension of Christ reminds us of an important truth for the Church. Our Lord's ascension suggests that there must always be an upward orientation in the life of the Church. We look up because He is above and will return from above. This does not demand that we be so heavenly minded that we are of little earthly good.

The preceding leads us to the realization that because the Lord of the Church is above, and since He is our standard of excellence, we must always be concerned about the quality of life in the Church. Eternal life must not be thought of as simply a quantity of endless time projected into the future, but it must be seen as a quality of life begun in time and continued in eternity at a higher plane.

This is an important consideration in keeping right perspectives for the Church, especially in an age when the earth-oriented devote themselves to the cult of success. What are some of the implications for the Church of this upward perspective?

First, the Church has a new *orientation*. In that epistle which portrays Christ as the Head of the Church, Paul writes: "If ye then be risen with Christ, seek those things which are above, where Christ sitteth on the right hand of God" (Col. 3:1). He then urges the Colossians to set their minds on the "above things." Such must constitute the Church's frame of reference. Deployed as she is on earth, deeply involved in preaching the Gospel, and ministering to the needs of man, her orientation must remain an upward one.

Paul penned these words to the unruly Corinthian fellowship: ". . .we look not at the things which are seen, but at the things which are not seen: for the things which are seen are temporal; but the things which are not seen are eternal" (II Cor. 4:18). The Church has a different standard for "success" and must be careful not to use the measurements of the seen world.

To simplify the matter Isaiah issues the warning that the ways and thoughts of God are not the ways and thoughts of man, and God will work through and bless His Word alone (Isa. 55:8-11). Thus, the Church must ever be on guard against allowing passing fads or religious gimmickry to usurp the teaching of Scripture.

Another implication for the Church in the ascension of Christ is that the Church is a new *organism*. The Church is not mere organization, but rather a living organism. When Christ ascended, the Spirit descended, and served as midwife at the birth of the Church. Thus, as a living organism, the Church was born to grow. At key junctures in Acts we find summary statements which verify such growth.

Acts 9:31 reveals that the Church "Throughout all Judea and Galilee and Samaria. . .continued to increase (grow)," following the conversion of Saul of Tarsus. But a different emphasis is seen in Acts 12:24, after the judgment on Herod, "But the word of the Lord continued to grow and to be multiplied"; and also after the Ephesian awakening as Acts 19:20 records, "So the word of the Lord was growing mightily and prevailing."

One observes in these passages a correlation between a growth in terms of human response and the impact of the declaration of the Word. We assume from earlier portions of Acts that numbers of people were being added to the Church on a regular basis. But one must quickly affirm that the basic word for growth in the New Testament, while encompassing agricultural, physical and spiritual growth, primarily is used in a qualitative sense. Paul sees a qualitative growth for the Church in Ephesians 2:20-22, as believers "grow into a holy temple in the Lord." He amplifies this with the forceful words found in Ephesians 4:13-15.

With its upward orientation in terms of a standard of excellence, and with a growth process in the Church which intimately and corporately relates the believer to his Lord, the Church therefore must keep before it a new *objective*.

Thus, Peter portrays the testing of spiritual growth as a possibility. Following one's incorporation into the Body of Christ via repentence and faith (Acts 2:37-38), there is to be growth, as the believer feeds first upon the milk and then the meat of the Word. Growth will be the spiritual litmus for both profession and possession of real spiritual life. In fact, Peter's last admonition to the troubled believers he addresses in his second epistle is "But grow in grace, and in the knowledge of our Lord and Savior Jesus Christ" (II Pet. 3:18a). Peter is exhorting the faithful to growth no matter what circumstances may be. That is the very nature of the Christian creature—growth. Yet this growth is clearly associated with internal quality, and not external quantity.

Paul reinforces this growth objective for the Church in his statements to the Colossians. His prayer for them at the commencement of that letter includes his desire that they bear fruit in every good work and grow in the knowledge of God (Col. 1:9-10). What is so significant here is that the apostle links the very purposes of God with the quality of life in the Christian. This concept is further borne out in the vital passage Colossians 2:19 in which Paul sees a growth for the Church which is uniquely from and of God.

Where does all of this lead us? It is pointing toward the importance of understanding what true Church growth is. The flood of books and seminars on the subject today seems to equate church growth with quantitative growth. The growing church will be a large church, crammed with people and programs, a veritable beehive of activity. Acts is alluded to in supporting this correlation between growth and numerical increase. What is never mentioned is that following the early acquisitions of converts, there was a Divine scattering in Acts 8 in which many of these people began to make their way home. The language of the New Testament does not support the multi-thousand type "churches" extant on the American scene. Neither does it oppose the same, but the details of the epistles do suggest small, rather than large fellowships.

The concern here is to emphasize that the preponderant use of the concept of growth in the early Church relates to qualitative growth in individuals, a growth then mirrored in the corporate life of the Church. We do well to quote Colossians 2:19 where Paul warns of the danger of "...not holding fast to the Head, from whom the entire body, being supplied and held together by the joints and ligaments, grows with *a growth which is from God.*"

We need to be aware of these cliche formulas for church growth which equate success with methods, men and multitudes of people. The Church must search the Word, and discover and recover that growth which is from God. With it there will be dynamic, without it there will be dilution. The Church must re-affirm its commitment to quality, and then thankfully receive that quantitative increase God gives.

A number of years ago I worked several summers in a company which produced adding machines. I sat at a bench doing quality control, working through trays containing masses of the same small part. The job required running the parts through a slot gauge, then determining, in my simplest terms, "Too thick, too thin, or just right."

But after hours of doing literally thousands of these parts, I sensed a confusion developing, so much so that the mere quantity befogged that simple test for quality. Anyone who has ever done this kind of monotonous factory work can understand the predicament. Simply put, quantity had confused my understanding of quality.

The Church in America faces that dilemma today. There is no excuse for stagnation in the local church, but neither is there merit in setting mere numerical goals as the measure for success. Paul sets the issue in perspective in writing to the Corinthians: "I have planted, Apollos watered; but God gave the increase. So then neither is he that planteth anything, neither he that watereth; but God that giveth the increase" (I Cor. 3:6-7).

In these days let the Church seek afresh the preeminence of the Word with its clear commitment to spiritual quality, and then see God bless with that quantitative increase pleasing to Him, and beneficial to the Church.

III. Antidote

Endangered Species

TWO NEW HAMPSHIRE COLLEGE PROFESSORS are studying the feasibility of restoring an interest in sheep raising in New England. In the mid-1800s there were, surprisingly, some 3 million sheep in Vermont and about 300,000 in western Massachusetts. A century later the statistics for the same areas were 8,000 and 6,000. The westward migration helped produce this eclipse in the sheep raising industry, but if you remember New England church history, you sadly recall that another kind of sheep has also dwindled in what was once America's Bible Belt.

A worker in the Vermont Department of Agriculture points out that, "Sheep are very dependent, like babies. You couldn't leave them alone, even in the Garden of Eden." Sheep, spiritually speaking, form the constituency of the Church. The history of the Church, in particular in North Africa and New England, indicates that this species is always an endangered one. Though the Scriptures point to the vulnerability of this flock, in so doing, they also reveal the measures to be taken to safeguard the sheep.

The late Dr. Barnhouse, in observing the increased emphasis on the intellect in the Church, wondered aloud if the admonition to "feed my sheep" had been changed to "feed my giraffes." Sheep raising remains that holy industry of the Church, and pastors and people alike need to reemphasize this task. Not only do the sheep wander away from the pews, but pastors also seem prone to wander from their pulpits to involve themselves in peripheral ego-building activity so typical of our day.

Some questions need to be raised about this endangered species. What is the nature of the species? It is, in fact, ever in danger. John 10, the Good Shepherd chapter, points this out. John 10:1 and 10 indicate the constant eixstence of thieves who seek to attack and destroy the sheep. What multiplied bands of brigands exist today to tear at the Church both from within and without! Conversely, verses 11, 14, and 15 reveal that sacrificial and sustaining love of the Lord for His sheep. He died for them on the cross, and He lives to intercede on their behalf.

Many of the ecclesiastical issues of the day are utterly marginal to that purpose for the sheep described by our Lord, "And other sheep I have, which are not of this fold: them also must I bring. . .and there shall be one fold, and one shepherd" (John 10:16). The other sheep doubtless were Gentiles, but there still are the other sheep of our day, and the Church must ever keep first its redemptive mission in the world. The Lord then went on to show that His death was to be the price paid for the gathering together of this one, multi-faceted flock (John 10:17-18).

What then is the need of this endangered species? Simply put, the sheep must be fed, and they must be led into the feeding areas of the Word. Because readers are so taken with the restoration of Peter in the John 21:15-17 passage, they tend to lose sight of the emphasis of the Lord upon the sheep. The flock is fragile. Three times the Good Shepherd rehearses this fact as He draws Peter back into the circle of usefulness. The words "feed my lambs" and the twice repeated "feed my sheep" warn us of the priority task of the pastors of local flocks.

Review some of the trends of recent years in the Church. Preoccupation with seminars, seeking experiences, and size of churches have beguiled many from the primary ministry, the exposition of the Word, and the feeding of the sheep. A generation of "Coke and French fries" Christians needs a diet of meat, basics from the Book!

Did the early Church discern its primary ministry? Peter himself would write later to the brethren with leadership responsibility in the local churches, "Feed the flock of God!" (I Pet. 5:2). In that passage Peter brings his apostolic authority to bear to admonish the overseers of the flocks to feed their charges, always setting an example in deed for what they conveyed in word.

It is not here intended to absolve the sheep, but what a crying need there is today for pastors to make a fresh commitment to the pastoral ministry. Granted, that ministry is demanding, and often frustrating, but pastors need to redirect their energies toward the people in the flock. They need to abandon so many of the tangents which preoccupy their time and make them unavailable for the rigors of sheep raising.

Not only Peter, but also Paul grasped the import of that mundane task of caring for the sheep. In that highly emotional scene recorded in Acts 20, Paul met with the Ephesian elders at Miletus. Luke wrote at the close of this meeting that the elders wept and sorrowed because, "They should see his (Paul's) face no more" (Acts 20:38).

But Paul had important concerns to express to these leaders of local fellowships. The gravity of his words in Acts 20:25-27 underline the import of his parting challenge in verses 28-31. These elders were first to guard their lives, and then the flock entrusted to them by the Holy Spirit. They were expressly told to feed the church of God "which he hath purchased with his own blood," verse 28. How similar these words are to those of the Good Shepherd in John 10.

Clearly, the elders must first be fed. That meant that their lives had to be directed toward learning the principles of the Word, and then relating them to people in the flock. Pastors today must have the courage to say no to those time-consuming activities which do not relate directly to feeding the sheep. Countless pastors are bogged down in a deluge of busy work which has little to do with the challenge of this passage in Acts.

Paul pointed to the dangers which awaited the sheep

in terms of external dangers (v. 29), and then internal dangers (v. 30). In so doing he assumes an authority which goes with the awesome responsibility of tending the flock. There will be times when disruptive elements, in terms of Acts 20:29-30, will have to be shown the door, lest they pillage and make mockery of the Body of Christ. There is so much sweetness and light abroad these days that church discipline is avoided lest someone's feelings be hurt. Yet little concern is manifest for the fact that the sheep are blood-bought, and must be safeguarded, not along narrow sectarian lines, but in terms of spiritual nurture and care. The man from Damascus then reminded the Ephesian elders of his own example, established over three years of faithful sheep raising in Ephesus (Acts 20:31).

The Ephesian elders were to be committed to the ministry of raising the sheep, and the centuries have not changed that priority. There is a perceptible restlessness among the sheep today. Battered by the world and bewildered by trends in the Church, they long for a deeper and more personal fellowship which mere bigness and busyness cannot provide. Programmed almost to distraction, the sheep are looking anew for pastors who will feed them and tend them in their hours of weakness and need.

Whatever the size of a church or the diversity of its ministry, it still remains a flock in the sight of the Good Shepherd. The devil wants to scatter the sheep, to single them out in isolation, and lead them astray. By its very nature the flock of God is fragile, but the

Shepherd is faithful, and He expects of His shepherds a comparable faithfulness.

This is basic to the life of the Church and the churches. Pastors must be feeding, and then feeders, even as Paul described that task, "Take heed therefore unto yourselves, and to all the flock. . .to feed the Church of God. . ." (Acts 20:28). There is no higher calling. All of the efforts and auxiliary agencies used to proclaim the Gospel eventually have their roots in the local church and are a reflection of the Church. Thus, the accomplishment of the redemptive purposes of the Church is directly in proportion to the spiritual vitality of the local flocks. That health, in turn, will always be in direct ratio to the feeding process engendered by faithful pastors caring for the sheep.

The writer of Hebrews gathers it all together in his benediction: "Now the God of peace, that brought again from the dead our Lord Jesus, that great shepherd of the sheep, through the blood of the everlasting covenant, Make you perfect in every good work to do His will, working in you that which is well pleasing in His sight, through Jesus Christ: to whom be glory for ever and ever. Amen" (Heb. 13:20-21).

Embodied Life

THE MOST NOTICEABLE DIFFERENCE between the Old and New Testaments centers in the fact that in the Old Testament the people came to the tabernacle and the temple in order to worship God, whereas in the New Testament God came into the people and they became the temples of God. The prophetic word about the Holy Spirit, "He is with you, He shall be in you," was fulfilled on the day of Pentecost. Thus, the worshippers were not restricted to one geographical location; the Lord had provided a multitude of mobile temples.

Of course there would develop the synagogue and then the local church, but inhabitation and mobility were to be the hallmarks of God's New Testament working through men. On Pentecost the Spirit indwelt men; in the persecution which followed Stephen's death, these Creator-inhabited creatures went everywhere, preaching the Gospel.

In the current concern about Body Life and the gifts of the Spirit, one does well to exercise caution lest he fall into the error of seeking to identify his gift in order that he may simply go out and do "his thing" spiritually. The emphasis must reside where Paul placed it: ". . .ye are builded together for an habitation of God through the Spirit" (Eph. 2:22). As a previous chapter points out, the priority must rest with the presence, not the presents of God.

The title of this chapter suggests a slightly different approach by pointing toward embodied life, God in man. Three basic concepts arise from this crucial matter. First, *the Church is the temple of God*. All of the approaches to ecclesiology are careful to show the varying shades of meaning for the word "church." There is the Church universal, the church local, and the church in the sense of a physical entity, a building. Peter reveals that individual believers are the building blocks of this new temple, "Ye also, as living stones, are built up a spiritual house. . ." (I Pet. 2:5). This being so, there is a supreme importance to the quality of these "stones," in particular as they relate to the structure of the local church.

There seems to be a preoccupation with the body count in attendance, rather than does the Body count in acceptable worship and service. Paul reinforces this teaching of Divine inhabitation in a two-fold fashion. In First Corinthians, the sixth chapter, he deals with a tragic moral problem in the fractured Corinthian fellowship. How could a Christian engage in fornication? Didn't they realize that God had actually taken up residence in them through the new birth experience? Because your body has now become "the temple of the Holy Spirit," you no longer have jurisdictional control over your life, no less your body. You have actually been purchased by the Lord, and the price was His shed blood. The closing words in this context (vv. 19-20) indicate far-reaching implications for our conduct inasmuch as we are to "glorify God...in body and in spirit." So Paul reasoned with them.

Many of us react strongly to a certain form of negativism which pervaded the Church a generation ago. We rebel against defining the Christian faith in negatives. Yet there are a host of negatives in the Scriptures; the commandments surely are an example of this. We want, especially in approaching the non-believer, to accent the positive. But the Scriptures make it clear that conversion and a change in life are spiritual corollaries. The Christian has to be different. Why? Because God lives in him.

In a previous chapter of this same epistle, chapter 3, Paul makes plain the fact that the local church is also the temple of God. This is a natural, or shall we say, supernatural confluence with the truth that the individual Christian is a mini-temple of God. In this context Paul is inveighing against the problems of schism and carnality, and he does so by pointing out that they bear a corporate responsibility for the affairs of this Corinthian church. Why? Because "The Spirit of God dwelleth in you" (I Cor. 3:16). In strong words Paul warns that the one who defiles the local temple will himself be defiled. There are isolated passages in the New Testament to indicate that what Luther called "the strange work of God," His judgment, could fall on recalcitrant members of the Church. Embodied life, individualistic at its core, is also corporate at its circumference. We are our brother's keeper in this unique God-inhabited fellowship.

Second, *the Church is the temple of God with a priesthood*. The writer of the epistle to the Hebrews focalizes the leadership for this human priesthood in the risen High Priest Jesus Christ. This High Priest has an unchanging ministry. The paradox of His priesthood is that He was both offerer and offering, as He submitted Himself to the cross, and with His final and perfect sacrifice made possible access to God apart from human intermediaries.

The basic requirement to be priests unto God under this High Priest is that such servants must receive not an office, but a nature, the very life of God in man. That pivotal Protestant doctrine of the priesthood of the believer is predicted on the basis of Peter's words in I Peter 1:18-19. Repentance and faith lead to the sealing work of the Spirit, and this rooted in "The precious shed blood of Christ, as of a lamb without blemish and without spot," the offering who was also the offerer. As the Book of Leviticus gives the Old Testament pattern for the priesthood, it emphasizes the importance of holiness. The word holy is frequently used in that book.

Therefore, this new priesthood centers not upon office, but rather upon origin, as Peter reminded these believers that they have been ". . .born again (from above), not of corruptible seed, but of incorruptible, by the word of God, which liveth and abideth for ever" (I

Pet. 1:23). We see a great difference between these Old and New Testament priesthoods, a moving from external to internal characteristics. Peter proceeds in the second chapter of this same epistle. "But ye are a chosen generation, *a royal priesthood*, an holy nation, a peculiar (set apart) people; that ye should shew forth the praises of him who hath called you out of darkness into his marvelous light" (I Pet. 2:9).

Peter immediately follows this panoply of descriptive terms of what believers in Christ are, with a series of admonitions concerning their conduct, their quality of life. The Levitical priesthood was set apart from and for the nation of Israel. Likewise, the New Testament priesthood demands an apartness from the world and unto God. One picks out these key phrases from I Peter 2:11-12, "...abstain from fleshly lusts...by your good works...glorify God. ..."

Today it's difficult to tell the saints from the sinners without a score card. We are in, but not of the world. We are to be insulated, though not isolated from the world. "World" is here used to connote a system of thought and life which is in rebellion against and alienated from God. One of the truths of Scripture which constantly guarded my conduct while facing the immorality and worldly practices of military duty in Japan was this concept, "That my body was the temple of the Holy Spirit." God actually lived within me. I was one of His priests. Christ in us, not only the hope of glory, but the harbinger of biblical holiness. What a lost chord in the Church today!

Finally, *the Church is the temple of God with a*

priesthood which offers spiritual sacrifices. The story is told of the rural visitor who attended a church in the big city. He was overwhelmed by the beauty of the service, quite a contrast from the simpler services in his small Baptist church. Somehow he had to express his appreciation to the minister in charge. Leaving the service, he blurted out, "Reverend, I sure did enjoy your form of lethargy this morning."

The word "liturgy" is actually transliterated into the English from the original, and it means "service." Sometimes as in the just cited illustration, we have the right thought but the wrong word. Paul, in coming to the application of his Roman epistle, blended sound thoughts with appropriate words. He saw the Christian as engaged in a continual spiritual liturgy or service. The believer also was the offerer and offering in terms of Romans 12:1, "I beseech you therefore, brethren, by the mercies of God, that ye present your bodies a living sacrifice, holy, acceptable unto God, which is your reasonable service (liturgy)."

In light of what God has done for us, the only rational response in terms of service is a living liturgy involving the submission of our bodies to His purposes. Immediately Paul advanced to the concept of apartness of life in Romans 12:2. Apartness from the world, "And be not conformed to this world," and apartness unto the Lord, "but be ye transformed by the renewing of your mind, that ye may prove what is that good, and acceptable, and perfect, will of God."

Therefore, embodied life means the vitality of God expressed through the vessels of believers, their bodies, who in corporate action form the Body of Christ. What we do with our bodies is significant in terms of Romans 12:1. One of the besetting sins in the Church goes unreproved—the sin of gluttony. Overweight Christians have little place for hurling judgment at some of the overt sins of others. The physical here reflects the inner spiritual discipline.

Peter spoke of offering spiritual sacrifices to the Lord. Specifically, what would these sacrifices be? The writer of Hebrews singles out words and deeds as being such sacrifices. He writes: "By him therefore let us offer the sacrifice of praise to God continually, that is, the fruit of our lips giving thanks to his name" (Heb. 13:15). That dangerous instrument, the tongue (James 3), can best be controlled by employing it in a positive vein. What better way to fill our conversation than with praise and thanks to the Lord.

Following this admonition concerning the verbal sacrifices, the writer directs us "To do good and to communicate forget not: for with such sacrifices God is well pleased" (Heb. 13:16). The believer priest can impact meaningfully in this world by directing his energies into the performance of good works, for the glory, and in the name of the Lord. This is neither do-goodism nor social activism, but rather the expression of the love of God to others in practical ways.

There is a place for such works in a structured fashion by the Church, but much more significant is it when it develops one to one from the spontaneous over-flow of a redeemed life! There are spheres of influence each believer-priest holds exclusively where his life can diffuse the light and life of the Gospel through good works. Such good works do not obtain, rather they explain the Gospel, and this was the thrust of James' letter to people whose religious experience was oriented toward religious verbalization. Let the Christian be as his Master, recognized as one who goes about doing good. Yet in such doing the opportunities arise for speaking the praises of what the Lord has done.

The genuine quality of sacrifice can be reflected in such word-deed sacrifices. The Church needs to ease off from its tendency to overorganize, and instead emphasize embodied life, inhabitation and mobility, each believer-priest going forth to share the redemptive message of the Gospel by word and deed. Such priests must be extremely conscious of Who indwells them. If even a small portion of the Church ever took seriously this matter of Divine inhabitation, it would "overturn" this world of ours in a generation. Rather, we seem more preoccupied with how and what rather than Who, and things rather than Him.

What a powerful concept. The Church is the temple of God with a priesthood which offers spiritual sacrifices. What tremendous responsibility, yet refreshing privilege resides in this concept of the embodied life!

Ears Movement

"IN ONE EAR AND OUT THE OTHER" is more than an archaic saying for the Christian. It reminds us that only a small portion of what is heard is retained. The parable of the sower further reveals the alarming fact that even the powerful Word of God brings varying degrees of response from those who hear it.

This is further magnified by the quantity of truth the Christian receives through sermons, services of all types, and personal Bible reading. Thus, we can better understand the force of the seven-fold repetition of the expression "He that hath an ear to hear, let him hear what the Spirit saith unto the churches." This repeated admonition to the churches of Asia Minor underscores the importance of truly "hearing" the Word of God. Our Lord also added a similar footnote to many of His parables by saying, "He that hath ears to hear, let him hear."

Obviously, listeners are equipped physically to hear, but do they really hear? No! Not all "hear" in terms of understanding what is said to them. Even so, the emphasis resides in the importance of hearing. In our age of internal and external noise pollution, the fine art of hearing is fast becoming a lost art.

The Christian desperately needs to recapture this skill, for the psalmist cites the high value of listening when he says, "Be still and know that I am God" (Ps. 46:10a). In the midst of constant clamor the place of stillness must be rediscovered. The Church today needs a new movement, though actually a return to an old one. Let it be called "The Ears Movement." We need a generation of believers who will make the effort to rest their jaws and exercise their ears anew in order to hear what the Spirit saith unto the church today.

Daniel would add to the words of the psalmist to produce a pattern for our times. "Be still and know that I am God." "the people that do know their God shall be strong and do exploits" (Dan. 11:32). A restive, modern generation wants to do exploits, before first being quiet and knowing God. Much of church activity is now verbal; in fact, an entire religious sub-culture has developed in the Church around that human organ so graphically described by James as being "untamable by man" (James 3:8).

Somehow we must declare a moratorium on man's talk, and allow God to speak again, but through His Word, and not the subjective experiences of men. The Church needs an environment of spiritual silence to hear anew the God-breathed Scriptures.

What is to be involved in this spiritual silence? There is first the *price of silence*. Simply put, it means that man must stop talking. Understand, this is not a call to dumbness. But if man is to hear God, he must be still and listen.

I will never forget the reaction of a visitor to a service I had just led. His comment, "You talk too much!" After recovering from the sting of the remark, I explored the man's reasoning and was amazed to realize that he was right. I had not given him time to quiet himself in order to hear God speak. What is true of a given service is true of much of our hectic church programming. Surely, St. Vitus is the patron saint of modern evangelicalism!

There are at least two payments involved in the price of silence. There must first be a *submission*. An interesting passage of Scripture portrays this. In Deuteronomy 15, Moses related the condition that the Hebrew, in servitude, was to be released in the seventh year. If that servant voluntarily chose to remain in the servant relationship, this procedure was to be followed: "Then thou shalt take an aul, and thrust it through his ear unto the door, and he shall be thy servant for ever. . ." verse 17. Being impaled for an instant to the door represented identification forever with that household. But why the ear? Was it not to indicate in symbol that the servant was the listener, the master was the authoritative speaker, and the ear was the instrument for receiving the commands? Today we need Christians with pierced ears, not for decorative reasons, but for discipleship purposes.

In paying the price of silence, there must also be a *sensitivity* to God's ways. Churches are noisy places these days. Our music, methods and manners bespeak sound and fury, but often signify nothing. The amen from the heart has been replaced by the applause of the hands, as the temple of God is slowly turning into a theater for men.

Elijah the prophet had seen Divine intervention in his contest on Mount Carmel with the prophets of Baal (I Kings 18). He was very much tuned to the dramatic. But he fell from the heights to the depths in his confrontation with the wicked Jezebel. In the nineteenth chapter of First Kings, we see the Lord graciously dealing with Elijah. Called forth from his place of hiding, Elijah is impressed by the great and strong wind, and the earthquake, and then the fire. However, the Lord did not communicate through those dramatic means; rather we read in verse 12, "After the earthquake a fire; but the Lord was not in the fire; and after the fire a *still small voice*."

What a lesson here for the multitudes today who look for the spectacular; the wind, earthquake, and fire, when they need to be still and listen for the quiet, empowering voice of God. If Elijah had to be quieted in order to hear, what of our generation?

What else is involved in spiritual silence? There is the *purpose for silence*. That purpose is to allow God to speak to man. The ancient preacher, though himself skilled with words, could write this warning to worshippers in the house of God, "Keep thy foot when thou goest to the house of God, and be more ready to hear, than to give the sacrifices of fools. . .Be not rash with thy mouth, and let not thine heart be hasty to utter any thing before God: for God is in heaven, and thou upon earth: therefore let thy words be few" (Eccles. 5:1-2).

The present day emphasis on gifts and lay participation in the Church is a welcome and needful one; but it has unwittingly contributed, in some situations, to a diminution of an authoritative proclamation of the Word. Thus, a crescendo of voices arises, while sound biblical exposition is frequently replaced with a pallid "sharing" of religious feelings and experiences; i.e., the voice of a man for the voice of God. Oh, for the heart of young Samuel, "And the Lord came, and stood, and called as at the other times, Samuel, Samuel. Then Samuel answered; Speak, for thy servant heareth" (I Sam. 3:10).

Samuel had to listen in order to hear. So we need to watch our step verbally. Does this emphasis on silence suggest some trend toward mystic contemplation? Such is not the intent. Mark, that out-of-breath Gospel writer, took the time to record some fifteen retirements of the Lord. These occasions reveal the priority our Lord placed on spiritual quietness. Thus, even the Son of Man needed to hear the Father speak, apart from the demanding voices of men.

Thirdly, we need to see the *prosperity from silence*. When man listens, and God speaks, then only blessing can be in store. David is a classic illustration of this. Shortly after his being anointed as king of Israel, David faced the the menacing incursions of the Philistines. Defeated once, the Philistines persisted in their efforts to overcome the Israelites, "And the Philistines yet again spread themselves abroad in the valley" (I Chron. 14:13).

Certainly decisive action was required of David at this juncture, but he is halted by the Lord, "And God said unto him, Go not up after them" verse 14. David was then told to assemble his forces near some mulberry trees, "And it shall be, when thou shalt hear a sound of going in the tops of the mulberry trees, that thou shalt go out to battle: for God is gone forth before thee to smite the host of the Philistines" verse 15. Some have inserted the words "the sound of marching" in the preceding verse. But either way the thought remains. Stop your activity and listen for the instruction of God; and then go out with the assurance that His presence goes with and before you.

That is our pattern in action: "Be still...and know... and do exploits." Instead of rushing off into battle, David obeyed the Lord, and the Scriptures recorded the result: "David therefore did as God commanded him: and they smote the host of the Philistines from Gibeon to Gazer" (I Chron. 14:16).

The preceding does indeed have the ring of orthodoxy to it, but what about the practical application of the same? Immediately one faces the dilemma of trying to program the speaking of God if one tries to establish a simplistic formula. But at least some suggestions can be made.

Central to the discussion is the presupposition that "all Scripture is God-breathed." Though we learn through the ways of God, in life, our source of truth is found in the Spirit-given Word of God, the Scriptures. Therefore, our churches must demand of pastors solid exposition and application of the Word. Sermons must be saturated with the Word, and not with cute stories and personal anecdotes.

Services of worship, and even teaching sessions, should allow for occasions of silence. We need to schedule more silence into our services. There is just too much man-originated talking going on, both from the pulpit and in the pews. Granted, one cannot produce a climate for listening through mere atmosphere, but we must afford busy modern man time to collect himself in preparation for true listening.

Allowing for the fact that many traditionalists have a decided bias against contemporary music, still we must ask ourselves, what is the justification for much of modern Christian music? Getting the congregation to clap their hands and tap their toes is hardly a heresy, but if the words do not carry significant biblical and spiritual substance, then that music fails of its purpose. The environment produced by such music would demand a shout, rather than a still small voice to penetrate the hearts and minds of those present.

When it comes to small groups and sharing times, we must guard against mere subjective talkathons. Too often experiences are given an exaggerated prominence over the Word of God. As Oswald Chambers so ably put it, "Experience as an end in itself is a disease; experience as a result of the life being based on God is health." One might well rephrase Paul's words in a new context, "Better to listen to and understand a few words of Scripture, which can empower one's life, than to hear a flow of verbal meanderings from human experiences."

One of the critical problems for Christians today in this area of hearing God speak through His Word centers in the multiplicity of activities in our churches. Spiritual maturity becomes confused with attending meetings. Most of our churches are overprogrammed, for we have come to reason that the active church is the alive church, but the brethren are so busily engaged on the treadmill of meetingitis that they hardly have the opportunity to digest and absorb the banquet of truths they hear, and soon we find ourselves producing, not saints, but saintlets.

Some churches have recognized this, and have made a start in the right direction by leaving at least one night a week free from scheduled activities. Churches have, and can, set aside certain weeks when services are restricted to Sunday and prayer meeting night. We must allow people time for their families, time for involvement in the community as witnesses, and above all, time for listening to the Lord. We can do this by scaling down the hectic pace of life we increase by our demands through excessive church programming.

All of the above relates also to the individual, but what else can he or she do to hear the voice of God through the din of modern life? Whatever happened to the personal devotional life? True, it can become a Pharisaical fetish, yet this is the touchstone of the problem. Individuals must cultivate their relationship to the Lord. Certainly there is no lack of books and helps, but the most important facet of one's "quiet time" is personal reading and study of the Scriptures.

Under the tutelage of the Holy Spirit, our lives would flourish if we would but take the time to develop this practice. A generation of believers which has made time for pro football can also take time for the Word.

Along with a personal renewal of Bible study, Christians would also do well to read the lives and works of those from the past who cultivated the listening habit. Bernard of Clairvaux, Brother Lawrence, David Brainerd, Oswald Chambers, and A. W. Tozer are but a few of those choice servants of God who were doers, because they were first hearers.

There are many other means of grace not dwelt on here, and prayer is one of them. But if we are to hear God today, we are going to hear Him preeminently through the Scriptures. Therefore, study of the Scripture needs to be both intensive and extensive. An overall grasp of Scripture would spare us from narrow peripheral views.

We must begin to schedule silence into our lives. Be it while jogging, bike riding, walking, or quietly sitting at home, we must begin to chew upon the truths we so abundantly hear. We must rethink and replan our lives, and reject the premise that we are too busy. Simply put, we must take time, whatever the cost, to hear what the Spirit has to say to us.

What a need in the Church today for the counterbalance of "The Ears Movement" and that silence which prepares us for service. The *price* of that silence is that man must be still before God and sensitive to His Word. The *purpose* for that silence is that God may speak through the Word. The *prosperity* from that silence will be that exploits will be done for the Lord.

Acts 21 records the apostle Paul's narrow brush with death at the hands of a frenzied Jerusalem mob. Having identified himself as a Roman citizen to the captain, Paul then beckoned to the crowd, indicating his desire to speak to them. Surprisingly, they granted him this opportunity, and the Scriptures give this description of that initial moment of meeting: "...And when there was made a great silence, he spake. . ." verse 40. What a strange way to describe the reaction of that crowd. "And when there was made a great silence. . ."

Could we lift those words from that historical moment and place them in our own? The Church, the churches, are filled with talk. Words cascade upon us, but so very much is the verbiage of man. We need "to make a great silence," to institute "The Ears Movement," and let the authoritative voice of God speak afresh through the Scriptures.

Then, with ears bathed and blessed by His truth, we can go forth from our retirements to enter the arena of life and do exploits for our God!

Energizing Goal

A VERY CLOSE CALL with a truck on I-80 outside of Youngstown, Ohio, led me to serious thinking as I returned home from taking my daughter to college in Illinois. A later-discovered carburetor problem had been that "trivial" factor which almost promoted me from time into eternity. Life and death always seem to ride on seemingly small matters.

But I was moved to consider life anew, and what the Church was doing with life, and lives. It seems as if the Church is taking cues from current life and allowing herself to become more and more complex. Yet it seems that the New Testament exudes an air of simplicity, without being simplistic. An observer of the religious scene has well written, "Religion, so far as it is genuine, is in essence the response of created personalities to the Creating Personality, God."

In Gospel terms the redeemed respond to the Redeemer through the blood-tie of Calvary. There a vital relationship is established, and this is the essence of faith, man in fellowship with God. Every generation since the fall has worked hard to confuse that simple fact. The orthodox, for all of their knowledge, seem most prone to this failing, for they are far too busy doing the work of the Lord to cultivate His friendship, after the pattern of Abraham, "the friend of God."

Really, shouldn't this relationship be simpler? It appears that there was a simple beginning. In the creation God said, "Let us make man in our image, after our likeness. . ." (Gen. 1:26). There follows in those first chapters of Genesis a picture of creation with a purpose. Man is to rule in the natural creation. He is to work in the Garden. Life, even before the Fall, was not intended to be one continuous fiesta/siesta situation. Man had satisfying and fulfilling tasks to accomplish within certain limits (Gen. 2:15-17).

What is of special interest is that the Creator was concerned that His creature, man, should have companionship, which He provided in Eve. One goes a step beyond this to wonder why God created man in the first place. With His foreknowledge and omniscience, God surely must have desired something unique, knowing from the outset what a troublemaker man would become.

But to return to this idea of God's concern that man not be alone, nor lonely, Genesis 2:18 speaks of this Divine concern. The next chapter records the tragic disobedience of Adam and Eve in the garden. Yet even in this account there is revealed the fact of that pristine fellowship between Creator and creature. "And they heard the voice of the Lord God walking in the garden in the cool of the day. . ." (Gen. 3:8). Some have suggested that in this is seen a pattern of God coming to commune with man on a regular basis. Thankfully, there were no traffic jams to fight through nor afternoon TV soap operas to distract the creature from this growing friendship with the Creator.

As there was a simple beginning, so there appears to be a simple ending. In the closing chapter of the Bible, we see the re-creation, paradise regained, so described in the early verses of chapter 22 of the Revelation. Verses 3 and 4 are of interest, for they follow through with the emphasis of Genesis. "And his servants shall serve him," (Rev. 22:3b). There will be gainful employment in heaven. As creatures we shall still be capable of learning, and such learning will enable us to fulfill those heavenly tasks.

Now to the real matter: "And they shall see his face; and his name shall be in their foreheads" (Rev. 22:4). To see His face is literally to see His person, for one's face is the characteristic image which comes to mind about another person. John said it a bit differently in his first epistle, "we shall be like him; for we shall see him as he is" (I John 3:2b). Because the very presence of sin will be removed from our spiritually metamorphosed bodies and beings, we shall be possessed of a limitless capacity to enjoy God and serve Him forever.

Does all of this sound too mystical and unreal? No! The unreality is in the St. Vitus' pace our churches exact of the sheep in the name of commitment. We are committing people to programs, projects, "progress," propaganda, prestige, but hardly to the priority of the Person of God, our Creator-Redeemer. The one who finds the open secret of fellowship with God will indeed be an active Christian but mere activity, conversely, will not guarantee the quality of inner life the Church desperately needs in her fellowship today!

There is no better place to turn than to the Psalms to see, in action, the working out of this simple principle about fellowship between God and man. Psalm 27 is especially helpful for it portrays a man in the heat and pressure of life still seeking that stabilizing factor of fellowship with the Lord. The very busyness and uncertainty of life drives David back to basics. First David speaks of the salvation which is his in the Lord, verses 1-3. Believed to have been written during the time that David had fled for his life from his rebellious son, Absalom, this portion of the psalm portrays David as being driven to that one invariable his situation afforded, "The Lord is my light and my salvation."

When everything else is collapsing in life, he still has this precious relationship to the Lord, therefore "Of whom shall I be afraid?" But this realization moves David from complexity to simplicity, for he longs for sanctuary with the Lord. In his topsy-turvy existence David is brought to the highest common denominator, "One thing have I desired of the Lord, that will I seek after. . ." verse 4. From the point of conversion, we move to the process of cultivation— cultivating the friendship of God. Dr. A. W. Tozer addressed himself on numerous occasions to the alarming fact that the whole transaction of conversion had been made mechanical and spiritless, as if some formula could automatically produce real saints. But he pointed out that, "Full knowledge of one personality by another cannot be achieved in one encounter."[1]

Thus David, who already knew the Lord, cried out his heart's desire, ". . .that I may dwell in the house of the Lord all the days of my life." And what is his purpose? "To behold the beauty of the Lord, and to inquire in his temple" (Ps. 27:4). There is a drive here, the most basic drive in man, that magnetism which draws the creature toward God. Granted, sin short circuits this in the unredeemed, but even he has the witness of conscience and nature to leave him sensing incompleteness and need. Security and joy come in His presence, so verses 5-6 further elaborate.

Christians of very strait and orthodox backgrounds seem drifting all over the ecclesiastical checkerboard nowadays, apparently looking for something extra and new. But what greater experience is there than that of finding Christ, and then questing to know Him better? This needs to be taught again, the seek-find-seek pattern of hungering and thirsting after the living God. Grounded in the sealing work of the Spirit in redemption, we launch out to cultivate the very friendship of God.

Will this tip us over into extremism? Hardly. Rather it will produce the fruit of the Spirit, and the orderly traits of the Sermon on the Mount, for our God is not the God of confusion.

As God hides David "in the secret of his tabernacle," verse 5, David develops a new sensitivity to the Lord. It focalizes in the words, "Thy face, Lord, will I seek," as seen in verses 7-10. David is obviously concerned about his conduct. He doesn't want anything to interrupt this sensitivity to the presence of the Lord. He may have been driven from the physical environs of the tabernacle, but he has discovered a fresh sense of God's presence which supersedes all other human relationships.

Again, these are not cries originating from some monkish isolation, but rather the words of one caught up in the very challenge of life. David closes the psalm with the practical application we need. "Teach me thy way, O Lord, and lead me in a plain path, because of mine enemies" (Ps. 27:11). Our world is just as real, and more pressurized than David's, thus we must know what God's unique purpose is for each of our lives. Whence is that derived? "Wait on the Lord: be of good courage, and he shall strengthen thine heart: wait, I say, on the Lord," verse 14.

This is not a plea to seek some esoteric truth nor some bizarre experience, it is a call to spiritual sanity. We must cultivate the friendship of God our Creator-Redeemer if our churches are to recapture that zest so patently a part of the early Church. This biblical mysticism, if it must be labeled, will deliver us from the drudgery and monotony of merely carrying on traditional programming and activity. The saints don't have to make that deadly choice between freezing or frying, cold orthodoxy or hot fanaticism.

We can be the kind of real people the lost need to see, with a zest for life and a freshness of spirit which delivers us from a cliche religious life.

Our churches can become premature paradises regained, if we focus on Him, and then His! Isn't that what Mark related? As he wrote of our Lord's calling of the twelve, he recorded these words, "And he ordained twelve that they should be with him, and that he might send them forth to preach" (Mark 3:14). It was first Him, "be with him," and then His, "sent forth to preach," being in the presence of the Lord, and then accomplishing the purposes of the Lord. Who would debate that the Church today has reversed that order?

Another Psalm adds the closing footnote to this discussion of the energizing goal for the Church and the individual Christian. "As the hart panteth after the water brooks, so panteth my soul after thee, O God. My soul thirsteth for God, for the living God: when shall I come and appear before God?" (Ps. 42:1-2). There is no more excruciating torment physically than intense thirst. Writing in a land where water was life, the psalmist here compares this thirst with that holy drive he experiences in desiring to know the Lord.

Our conveyor belt approach to the souls of men leaves few with such a thirst. In fact, we discourage such a drive. But individuals, in the privacy of their relationship to the Lord, will herald publically in a simple and quiet way the vitality we cannot program into our church life. Fed from the totality of the Scriptures, where Christ is revealed, (John 5:39) individuals will commend the Gospel to the unbelieving world, and enable ecclesiastical deserts to blossom as the rose.

As this effort began with fiction, so it shall end with the balance of fact. No, there is no perfect church in the ultimate sense of that word, but there can be a perfect, mature church, reflecting the Face of God, though through the frailty of men. Such a church is discovered in the pages of the Book of Acts, a church of realistic greatness, born of the Spirit, and then borne along by that selfsame Holy Spirit of God. Such a "perfect" church is described in the epilogue which follows.

---

1. A. W. Tozer, *The Pursuit of God*, (Harrisburg: Christian Publications, Inc., 1948), p. 13.

Epilogue

The Marks of a
Great Church

ONE OF THE THEMES which keeps recurring in Christian publications relates to the concept of what constitutes a "great" church. Two of the factors which continually rise to the surface indicate that size and program rank high in modern day appraisals of church greatness. The Book of Acts certainly reveals that the word "great" does have a numerical flavor, but it goes beyond numbers to reveal a correlation with the glory and power of God.

Of real interest is the fact that Acts literally describes what a "great church" is by the very use of that expression in a definite way. Thus, we should find it most profitable to discern a seven-fold description of a great church from the pages of Acts. As we progress through the early chapters of this book, we see the characteristics of biblical greatness for a church.

In Acts 4:33 we read: "And with *great power* gave the apostles witness of the resurrection of the Lord Jesus . . ." One's mind immediately turns to Acts 2 and the day of Pentecost when divine power, through the person of the Holy Spirit, took up residence in human vessels. The waves of impact from that event surged right to the close of Acts.

The dynamite of God kept exploding in human lives, so much so that the religious hierarchy recognized in the apostles an authority beyond their own (Acts 4:12-13). The power worked internally in the prayer life of the early church (Acts 4:31), and then externally in preaching the message of the resurrection. But this was personal power with a purpose—to win lost souls to the Savior-Lord.

Such power was not to be expended profligately in the quest for the bizarre and unusual experientially, but rather to confront a pagan, pseudo-religious world with the claims of Christ. Even the miraculous demonstrations of power were given to the same end—to verify the authority of the message, not the uniqueness of the messengers.

As the first part of Acts 4:33 spoke of the great power which swelled forth from the preaching of the Gospel, so the last portion of the verse describes the inner effect, "and *great grace* was upon them all." The beauty of the character and the glory of God were reflected in the lives of the believers. Not only was there the power of the Holy Spirit, there was also the fruit of the Spirit.

Twentieth century Christianity is so much exercised in seeking power that it has become careless about the necessity for holiness of life. The diversified, yet unified fruit of the Spirit of Galatians 5 addresses itself to the basic relationships of life: to God, to other men, and to ourselves. In Acts 4, Luke spoke of the sanctifying grace which changes lives, a concept somewhat lost in these days of instants.

Between the extremes of false fire and wild fire, there is to burn that Holy Spirit within who backs up our witnessing with our living. Quantity will never supersede quality in the sight of God. Dr. Vance Havner once described the typical Sunday morning congregation in these terms: "The clock struck twelve, and the church gave up her dead."

Such was not so in Acts; thus we should not be surprised at what happened in Acts 5. The spiritual temperature was such that the satanic germ warfare of sin was dealt with instantly.

In the temporary situation created by the vast number of believers in Jerusalem following Pentecost, there emerged the mysterious and awesome circumstances described in Acts 5:1-11, in which the divine justice dispatched Ananias and Sapphira.

Someone has well observed that the act of divine wrath is not so perplexing as the climate of holiness in the church which necessitated their deaths. In Acts 5:5 and 11, there is mentioned the *great fear* which came upon both the believers and the fringe element, those who were rather taken with this new phenomenon of "the way."

In an age which has deified man and humanized God, we sense the need for a revival of a wholesome biblical fear of God. Such seems lost in a day when our attempts to make God relevant to modern man have instead made Him irrelevant.

The atmosphere of our churches is becoming so man-centered and entertainment-oriented that the saints now must be amused and not amazed. Obviously, a church whose quality of life could keep the world at arm's length (Acts 5:13) would clearly be a church destined for trouble.

Another characteristic of the early church was the fact that it provoked opposition. People get so excited these days when some celebrity compliments God, but the celebrities in Luke's time were anything but complimentary.

Therefore, at the conclusion of Stephen's address, we see that mocking, threats, and beatings were replaced by martyrdom. Acts 8:1 states "And at that time there was a *great persecution* against the church ..." The quality of life, focalized in Stephen, demanded a response from the world and Stephen sealed his testimony with his blood.

But his death only expanded the declaration of the Gospel, touching as it did the angry Saul, fulfilling the plan of Acts 1:8 with the events of Acts 8:1, and then seeing the wrath of men used to the praise of God, as Acts 8:4 records, "Therefore, they that were scattered abroad went everywhere preaching the word."

As a pastor of a church in comfortable, affluent America, I am incapable at present of addressing myself to the message of suffering in I Peter or to this persecution in Acts 8. But the handwriting is on the wall for our land, and suffering is sure to be our portion. We need to be purged of the idea that the Gospel makes for popularity. The winnowing winds of persecution may soon cause a reassessment of our building plans as the wheat and chaff are separated in the churches.

This characteristic of sorrow follows logically and contextually from the preceding. "And devout men carried Stephen to his burial, and made *great lamentation* over him" (Acts 8:2). There is no contradiction here with Paul's teaching that "to be with Christ is far better." Rather, there is portrayed in Stephen's funeral the depth of love within the early church. The caliber of Stephen's life was such that he was sorely missed because he had been deeply loved by the church.

There is a "time to weep," to mourn for our Stephens, but in a climate of noninvolvement we seldom experience the kind of fellowship common to the early church. Our busyness has left us bankrupt in the area of true Christian friendships and fellowship. Some of our churches need to call a moratorium on program and get back to majoring on people.

Paradoxically, the occasion of sorrow became the vehicle for joy. Philip went forth to the city of Samaria (Acts 8:1), very much in the spirit of Psalm 126:6, "He that goeth forth and weepeth, bearing precious seed, shall doubtless come again with rejoicing, bringing his sheaves with him."

Philip, sobered and softened by persecution and sorrow, preached the Gospel to the half-breed Samaritans (an event of great implications itself); and so we read in Acts 8:8, "And there was *great joy* in that city."

What else could there be for those who sat in darkness, when the light of the Gospel shone in upon them? The risen Savior-Lord was declared, and many came to the genuine joy of a personal relationship to the living God.

Does this not show us a divine pattern? God sovereignly empowers men. His Holy Spirit breathes a new quality of life within them. Such holy life demands a confrontation with sin. The world then seeks to repulse this challenge to its domain, but the worst it can do simply deepens the life of the church, and then, through such as Philip, produces a new boldness to preach the Gospel.

If the believers in Jerusalem were surprised that Samaritans were being saved, even more amazing was the word which came from Gentile Antioch to the north. Propelled forth by the persecution, the believers saw a great harvest among pagan Greeks. "And the hand of the Lord was with them; and a *great number* believed, and turned unto the Lord" (Acts 11:21).

Though this spiritual harvest only increased the minority of Christians, yet God had blessed His Word with a "great number." Thus, we should expect to see lives changed and numbers of people coming to Christ. However, the delusive concept that greatness lies in statistical increase is devastating if the above is taken out of the total pattern we have seen developed in the Book of Acts.

In a culture saturated with instants, in a society where people want something not tomorrow, not today, but yesterday, it is a tempting prospect to desire